Arizona

by Thomas K. Adamson

Consultant:
Dawn M. Cromwell
Senior Education Program Coordinator
Arizona State Museum
The University of Arizona
Tucson, Arizona

Capstone press
Mankato, Minnesota

Capstone Press
151 Good Counsel Drive • P.O. Box 669 • Mankato, Minnesota 56002
http://www.capstone-press.com

Library of Congress Cataloging-in-Publication Data
Adamson, Thomas K.
    Arizona/by Thomas K. Adamson.
    p. cm.—(Land of liberty)
    Includes bibliographical references and index.
    Contents: About Arizona—Land, climate, and wildlife—History of Arizona—
Government and politics—Economy and resources—People and culture.
    ISBN 0-7368-1571-6 (hardcover)
    1. Arizona—Juvenile literature. [1. Arizona.] I. Title. II. Series.
F811.3 .A33 2003
979.1—dc21   2002011786

Summary: An introduction to the geography, history, government, politics,
    economy, resources, people, and culture of Arizona, including maps, charts,
    and a recipe.

Editorial Credits
Kremena Spengler, editor; Eric Kudalis, product planning editor; Jennifer
    Schonborn, series and book designer; Angi Gahler, illustrator; Kelly Garvin,
    photo researcher

Photo Credits
Cover images: Grand Canyon, Digitial Stock; saguaro cacti in Saguaro National
    Park, James P. Rowan

Arizona State Library, Archives and Public Records, Archives Division, Phoenix,
39, 45; Capstone Press/Gary Sundermeyer, 54; Corbis, 32, 38; Corbis/Bettmann,
26, 40; Corbis/Clive Druett, 19; Corbis/David Muench, 12; Corbis/Tom Bean,
34; Houserstock/Dave G. Houser, 48, 63; Houserstock/Jan Butchofsky, 42;
Houserstock/Tim Baldridge, 4; Hulton Archive by Getty Images, 23, 28, 31, 58;
James P. Rowan, 14-15, 24-25; Kay Shaw, 56, 57; Lissa Funk, 46–47; Pat &
Chuck Blackley, 8; One Mile Up, Inc., 55 (both); Tom Till, 1, 16, 20; U.S. Postal
Service, 59; Will Funk, 52–53

Artistic Effects
PhotoDisc, Inc., Corbis

1 2 3 4 5 6 08 07 06 05 04 03

Table of Contents

Chapter 1   About Arizona 5

Chapter 2   Land, Climate, and Wildlife 9

Chapter 3   History of Arizona 21

Chapter 4   Government and Politics 35

Chapter 5   Economy and Resources 43

Chapter 6   People and Culture 49

Maps   Arizona Cities .7
        Arizona's Land Features 11

Features   Recipe: Fruit Salsa 54
            Arizona's Flag and Seal 55
            Almanac 56
            Timeline 58
            Words to Know 60
            To Learn More 61
            Internet Sites 61
            Places to Write and Visit 62
            Index 64

With its red, purple, and brown rocks, the Grand Canyon is a breathtaking sight.

Chapter 1

About Arizona

Colorful rock shapes rise from the deep gorge of the Grand Canyon in northern Arizona. Visitors can stand on the canyon's edge to view the red, purple, and brown rock. At the bottom, 1 mile (1.6 kilometers) below, lies the Colorado River. Over millions of years, this fast-flowing river carved the steep cliffs to form the rocky display.

More than 5 million people hike and camp in the Grand Canyon every year. Many visitors go white-water rafting down the river's fast-moving rapids. People can ride mules to the canyon's bottom.

People can view the Grand Canyon from the South Rim or the North Rim. These sides of the canyon are only about

10 miles (16 kilometers) apart. But no roads cross the Grand Canyon. To get from one side to the other by car is a 215-mile (346-kilometer) trip. The South Rim is open year-round. The North Rim is open only during summer. Heavy snows prevent people from reaching the North Rim in winter.

The Grand Canyon is Arizona's most famous attraction. It gives Arizona its nickname, the Grand Canyon State.

Hot Deserts and Snowy Mountains

Arizona's landforms and weather contrast sharply. Arizona has canyons, deserts, mountains, and flat-topped rock mesas. The state capital, Phoenix, receives less than 10 inches (25 centimeters) of rain each year. Just 136 miles (219 kilometers) away in the mountains, Flagstaff can get several feet of snow in winter.

Arizona is in the southwestern United States. California and Nevada lie to its west. Utah is to the north, and New Mexico is to the east. Mexico borders Arizona to the south.

Arizona Cities

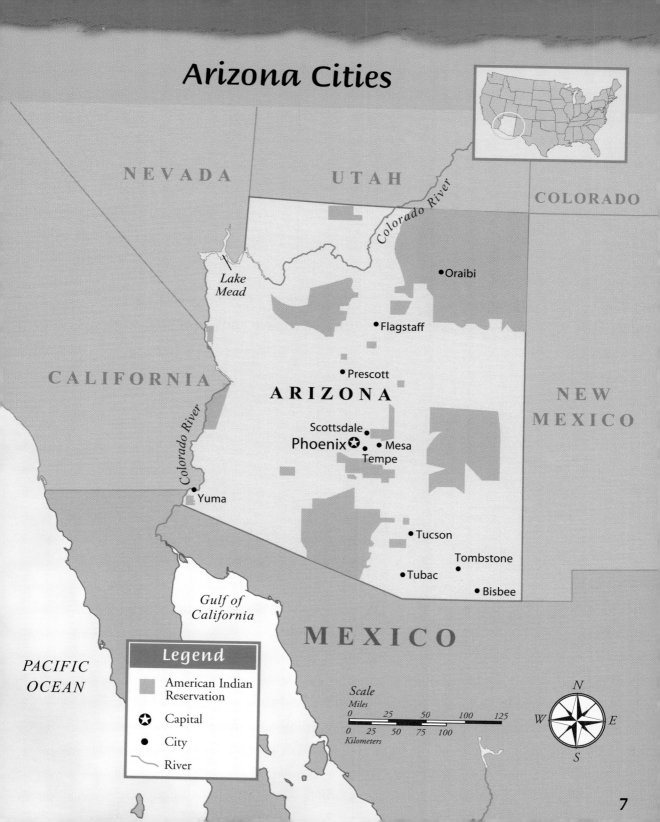

NEVADA

UTAH

COLORADO

Colorado River

Lake Mead

•Oraibi

•Flagstaff

CALIFORNIA

ARIZONA

•Prescott

NEW MEXICO

Colorado River

Scottsdale
Phoenix ✪ •Mesa
Tempe

•Yuma

•Tucson

Tombstone
•

•Tubac

•Bisbee

Gulf of California

MEXICO

PACIFIC OCEAN

Legend

⬛ American Indian Reservation

✪ Capital

• City

〰 River

Scale

Miles
0   25   50   100   125

0   25   50   75   100
Kilometers

N
W   E
S

Huge red rocks form the landscape of Monument Valley Navajo Tribal Park in northern Arizona and southern Utah.

Chapter 2

Land, Climate, and Wildlife

People visit different parts of Arizona depending on the weather. When it is hot in the desert, people visit the cool mountains. When it is cold in the mountains, they visit the warm desert.

Land regions in Arizona include the Colorado Plateau, the Transition Zone, and the Sonoran Desert.

Colorado Plateau

The Colorado Plateau lies in northern Arizona. This high, mostly flat area has some of the most colorful rocks in North America. Millions of years ago, rivers dumped huge trees on the plateau. The trees turned into red, orange, and green rock. Today, people can see these trees in the Petrified Forest. The nearby Painted Desert has rocks that appear to be painted red, purple, brown, and orange.

Monument Valley is on the Navajo Indian Reservation in the northern part of the plateau. Huge flat-topped rocks rise above the flat desert. Millions of years of wind and rain created these giant buttes and mesas.

The Colorado River cuts through the Colorado Plateau. It carves one of the most famous places in the world, the Grand Canyon.

The San Francisco Peaks rise above the Colorado Plateau near Flagstaff. They can be seen from more than 100 miles (160 kilometers) away. At 12,633 feet (3,851 meters) above sea level, Humphreys Peak is the highest point in Arizona.

Flagstaff receives an average of 8 feet 4 inches (2.6 meters) of snow each year. People enjoy challenging ski runs at the Arizona Snowbowl just north of Flagstaff.

Arizona's Land Features

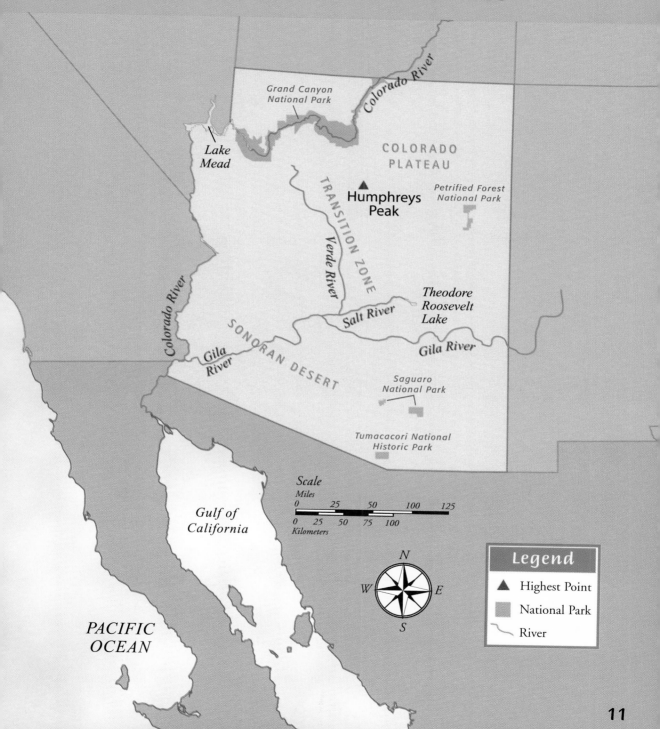

Grand Canyon
National Park

Colorado River

Lake
Mead

COLORADO
PLATEAU

▲
Humphreys
Peak

Petrified Forest
National Park

TRANSITION ZONE

Verde River

Colorado River

Gila
River

SONORAN DESERT

Salt River

Theodore
Roosevelt
Lake

Gila River

Saguaro
National Park

Tumacacori National
Historic Park

Scale
Miles
0   25   50   100   125
0 25 50 75 100
Kilometers

Gulf of
California

N
W   E
S

Legend

▲ Highest Point

⬛ National Park

〰 River

PACIFIC
OCEAN

The Salt River flows through Arizona's White Mountains, carving the Salt River Canyon.

The Mogollon Rim marks the southern boundary of the Colorado Plateau. This steep wall is nearly 2,000 feet (610 meters) high in some places. It extends more than 200 miles (322 kilometers) from Flagstaff to the border of New Mexico. The land drops down at the Mogollon Rim to the desert areas south of the plateau. On top of the rim is the largest ponderosa pine forest in North America. The Mogollon Rim has cooler weather than the desert.

Transition Zone

The Transition Zone is a narrow strip of land southwest of the Colorado Plateau. While the land of the Colorado Plateau is flat, the Transition Zone is mountainous. Several mountain ranges are close together in this rocky region.

The White Mountains in eastern Arizona are part of the Transition Zone. These high mountains include the Blue Range Primitive Area. Vehicles are not allowed into this 173,762-acre (70,321-hectare) region of mountains, pine forests, and steep canyons. Visitors either hike or ride horses to explore the area.

The Salt River Canyon cuts through the White Mountains. A highway runs down one side of the canyon and up the other side. This winding road provides a beautiful view of the steep-walled canyon. People can pull over and enjoy the scenery. They can also go white-water rafting on the Salt River.

Sonoran Desert

The Sonoran Desert covers much of southwestern Arizona. This desert also reaches into southeastern California and northern Mexico. Summer temperatures in the Sonoran Desert region often rise above 100 degrees Fahrenheit (38 degrees Celsius). The region receives less than 12 inches (30 centimeters) of rain each year.

Different kinds of cactus make this area colorful. The giant saguaro (suh-WAH-ruh) cactus grows only in this desert. This cactus can grow to more than 50 feet (15 meters) tall. It lives

for about 75 years before growing branches that look like arms. The saguaro cactus appears on Arizona's license plates. Javelinas, foxes, squirrels, and birds eat the fruit of the saguaro cactus. The fruit ripens in June and July. Other common types of cactus include the hedgehog, prickly pear, and barrel cactus.

Arizona's largest city, Phoenix, is in this region. People call the area around Phoenix the Valley of the Sun. They have adapted to living in the hot dry desert. Almost every house and building has air conditioning. People have built many

Saguaro cacti grow in the Sonoran Desert of southwestern Arizona.

Beavertail cacti have adapted to the hot, dry climate of the Arizona deserts.

dams to create lakes called reservoirs. Canals bring water from the reservoirs to the city.

Climate

For most of the year, the heat in the desert is dry. Temperatures can rise over 100 degrees Fahrenheit (38 degrees Celsius). In these high temperatures, the sun can be dangerous. In summer, it only takes 10 to 15 minutes for skin to become sunburned.

Arizona's wet season comes in July and August. The state receives more rain at that time of year than during any other two-month period. The air is more humid. Extra moisture in the air makes the heat even more unbearable. Thunderstorms can suddenly form and dump rain on some parts of the desert. The dry ground may not soak water quickly enough. The water may run off and cause flash floods.

After the rainy season, the weather cools off for winter. In winter, high temperatures can reach 70 degrees Fahrenheit (21 degrees Celsius). At night, they can drop below freezing.

Arizona's mountains are cooler than the desert. The summer high temperatures are between 70 and 80 degrees Fahrenheit (21 and 27 degrees Celsius). People who live in the Phoenix area sometimes travel to the mountains during summer to escape the heat. In winter, snow falls in the mountains.

Wildlife

Wildlife in the Sonoran Desert has adapted to the climate. Gila (HEE-luh) monsters can live for several weeks without eating. They store fat in their tails.

Many kinds of rattlesnakes live in Arizona, including ridgenose rattlesnakes. The ridgenose rattlesnake, Arizona's state reptile, lives in the southeastern part of the state. It eats rodents, lizards, and centipedes. It is small for a rattlesnake. It grows up to 2 feet (61 centimeters) in length.

Roadrunners sometimes run along roads in the desert. These birds cannot fly very well, so they prefer to walk or run. Quick-moving roadrunners can catch rattlesnakes to eat.

Javelinas live in Arizona's deserts. They look like pigs, but they are more slender and have longer legs. Javelinas have large heads and long snouts. They are usually dark gray with bristly hair.

Coyotes live throughout Arizona. Coyotes look like wild dogs but have bushier tails and longer ears. They eat rabbits and rodents.

The Gila monster is a poisonous lizard native to Arizona. Gila monsters use their poison to defend themselves. Gila monsters have strong jaws and their bites can go half an inch (1.25 centimeters) deep. Gila monsters eat bird eggs, baby birds, baby mice, and frogs.

The ringtail is Arizona's state mammal. It is about the size of a cat but has larger ears and eyes. The ringtail actually belongs to the raccoon family. The animal gets its name from its long black-and-white striped tail. It is most active at night and lives in rocky areas or canyons.

Pollution

Arizona's air and land are affected by pollution. On some days, a brown haze hangs over Phoenix. Gases and dust particles from cars cause the haze. Since there is little wind in Phoenix, the haze seems to hang in the sky. People are looking for ways to solve the air pollution problem.

The ancient Anasazi people built these houses in the cliffs of northeastern Arizona.

Chapter 3

History of Arizona

Arizona became a U.S. state in 1912, but its history goes back much further. The native people who lived in what is now Arizona between A.D. 800 and A.D. 1400 did not leave any written records. Scientists learn about these people by studying the ruins and objects left behind.

Early Native Peoples

The two main groups of early native people were the Anasazi and the Hohokam. The Anasazi lived on the Colorado Plateau in northeastern Arizona. The Anasazi are probably ancestors of the Hopi Indians. The Hohokam lived in the central and southern Arizona deserts. These farmers built canals to bring water from the Salt River to their fields in the desert. The Pima and Tohono O'odham Indians are probably descended from the Hohokam.

The Anasazi and Hohokam disappeared by the 1400s. Scientists think a long dry spell may have occurred in the area and forced them to either leave or die from hunger.

In the 1400s, the Navajo and the Apache came to Arizona. The Navajo lived in the northeast. They grew crops and raised sheep. The Apache were hunters and lived in the mountains to the south.

Spanish Settlers

The Spanish were the first Europeans to explore the southwestern part of North America. From 1540 to 1542, Francisco Vasquez de Coronado led a group to search for the Seven Cities of Cibola. The Spanish thought these cities were made of gold. This belief turned out to be only a legend.

One of Coronado's men, Garcia Lopez de Cardenas, explored farther into Arizona. He became the first European to see the Grand Canyon. He was disappointed because he was looking for cities made of gold.

In the late 1500s, the Spanish began to settle present-day Arizona and New Mexico. Spanish missionaries moved into the area to bring Christianity to the American Indians. Most Indians did not want to give up their beliefs. The Indians thought the missionaries were trying to destroy their way of life. In 1680, the Hopi and other Pueblo Indians fought the Pueblo Revolt. They forced the Spanish to leave the area.

Some Spanish missionaries in Arizona wanted to help the American Indians. Father Eusebio Francisco Kino arrived in Arizona in 1691. He lived with the Pima in southern Arizona.

From 1540 to 1542, Francisco Vasquez de Coronado explored present-day Arizona and New Mexico.

Father Kino taught the Indians different ways to farm. He brought horses, sheep, mules, and cattle to the region. Father Kino died in 1711.

Other missionaries were not as helpful to the Indians as Kino. The Pima attacked some of the missions. The attack led the Spanish to build a military fort in 1752. Called Tubac, it was just south of today's Tucson.

Becoming Part of the United States

In 1821, Mexico declared its independence from Spain. At that time, Mexico included all of New Mexico and Arizona and parts of Colorado, Utah, Nevada, and California.

From 1846 to 1848, the United States and Mexico fought the Mexican War. The two countries disagreed over land claims. The war ended with the Treaty of Guadalupe-Hidalgo.

In 1797, Spanish missionaries completed Mission San Xavier del Bac near Tucson. One of the best known missions in Arizona, it is still in use today.

Wyatt Earp

Wyatt Earp (1848–1929) was born in Monmouth, Illinois. As a young man, Earp worked as a buffalo hunter. During the 1870s, he was a police officer in Wichita and Dodge City in Kansas. Earp moved to Tombstone, Arizona, in 1879. He worked as a stagecoach guard, card dealer, and deputy U.S. marshal.

In 1881, a quarrel developed between Ike Clanton's family and three of the Earp brothers, Wyatt, Virgil, and Morgan. Each side accused the other of links to bank robberies and horse thefts. In October, the Earps and their friend Doc Holliday shot three Clantons to death in the famous Gunfight at the O.K. Corral. The Earps said they were trying to make an arrest. Others said it was murder. Wyatt was tried in court and found not guilty. Later, Wyatt worked as a saloonkeeper and prospector.

The treaty called for Mexico to give part of its land to the United States for $15 million. This treaty gave most of Arizona to the United States.

One small area of land in southern Arizona was still part of Mexico. In 1854, the United States bought this piece of land for $10 million. The agreement was called the Gadsden Purchase. This purchase made the 48 connected United States appear as they do today.

The Wild West

Arizona became a U.S. territory in 1863. Many people in the country thought Arizona had no value. The people who lived there tended to settle arguments violently. Arizona was the classic Old West. Gunfights and train robberies were common.

The white settlers fought with the American Indians. The Apache and Navajo fought to keep their homelands. In 1863, Colonel Kit Carson and his troops forced several thousand Navajo to march 300 miles (483 kilometers) from Arizona to New Mexico. Many Navajo died during this march. The Navajo called it the "Long Walk."

In the late 1800s, the wars between American Indians and settlers in Arizona were coming to an end. A band of Apaches led by Cochise fought the U.S. Army in southern Arizona. Cochise never lost a battle, but he realized that the poorly-armed, outnumbered American Indians could not win the war. He surrendered in 1872. Another legendary

Geronimo, pictured on the right, led a small Apache band against thousands of U.S. soldiers.

warrior, Geronimo, led a small Apache band against thousands of soldiers. Geronimo finally surrendered in 1886.

In 1900, the population of Arizona was 124,000. Ten years later, it had increased to 206,000. Arizona was beginning to change its "Wild West" image. State militia, called the Arizona Rangers, helped track down and arrest criminals. The territory now seemed like a safe place to live.

Arizona adopted a state constitution in early 1911. The constitution allowed voters to call back all elected officials, including judges. Congress approved statehood for Arizona in August 1911. But President William Howard Taft strongly opposed the recall of judges. He did not allow Arizona to become a state until its constitution changed. Arizona voters approved the changes in late 1911. Arizona became the 48th state on February 14, 1912. It was the last of the connected 48 states to join the Union.

Water and Heat Issues

Water is always a concern in the desert. People need drinking water, and farmers need water to irrigate their fields. In 1911, Arizona completed the first project to bring water to the desert. Roosevelt Dam was built on the Salt River. In 1996, builders raised the height of the dam by 77 feet (23 meters) and increased the size of Roosevelt Lake.

Seven states share water from the Colorado River. Arizona, California, Utah, Nevada, New Mexico, Wyoming, Colorado, and the U.S. government created the Colorado River Compact in 1922. This agreement decided how much of the river's water each state could use. Arizona uses 2.8 million acre-feet of Colorado River water each year. One acre-foot is 325,851 gallons (1.2 million liters). An acre-foot is the average amount of water a family of four uses in a year.

The population of the new state continued to grow. In 1934, A.J. Eddy of Yuma invented a device that enabled people to cool off their homes and businesses. The evaporative

Built in 1911, Roosevelt Dam on the Salt River brought water to the desert.

cooler helped people to deal with the extreme heat of summer. More people moved to the state.

World War II

During World War II (1939–1945), the U.S. military built bases in Arizona deserts. They used the flat open spaces to test

Two internment camps for Japanese Americans were built in Arizona during World War II.

weapons and aircraft. Many troops trained in Arizona. After the war, some of them returned to live in the state.

During World War II, many Japanese Americans were held prisoner in two Arizona internment camps. The Japanese military had attacked Pearl Harbor in December 1941. The U.S. government thought the camps were necessary for national security. The Colorado River Relocation Center near

Poston, Arizona, held as many as 18,000 Japanese Americans. As many as 13,000 were held at the Gila River Relocation Center near Sacaton, Arizona. At the time, these two camps were the third and fourth largest cities in the state, after Phoenix and Tucson.

Arizona after World War II

After retiring, many people from northern and eastern states moved to Arizona to enjoy the warm weather. Businessman Del Webb built a town called Sun City in the 1960s. The town was set up just for retired people. Sun City is northwest of Phoenix and has a population of about 40,000.

Construction of the Central Arizona Project began in 1973. It was completed in the early 1990s. This project brought water from the Colorado River to the deserts of southern Arizona. It includes 336 miles (541 kilometers) of pipelines that go to the area around Phoenix and reach as far south as Tucson. The entire project cost more than $4 billion.

Arizona lawmakers meet at
the state capitol in Phoenix.

Chapter 4

Government and Politics

The Arizona state government is organized like the federal government. It includes the executive, legislative, and judicial branches.

The governor heads the executive branch. The governor may serve any number of four-year terms. But the governor is not allowed to serve more than two terms in a row. Arizona has no lieutenant governor.

The legislative branch makes laws for the state. The legislature is divided into the senate and house of representatives. The 30 senate and 60 house members serve two-year terms.

"In Arizona, we have a record of putting differences aside to accomplish change for the greater good."
—Jane Hull, governor of Arizona from 1998 until 2002

The judicial branch is Arizona's court system. The highest court is the state supreme court. The governor appoints five justices to six-year terms.

Arizona voters usually support the Republican Party. In every presidential election since 1952, except for 1996, most Arizonans have voted for the Republican candidate. Maricopa County, where Phoenix is located, has the majority of the state's population. This county is important in elections. The Phoenix area usually votes Republican.

Arizona Politicians

Arizona has produced some unusual politicians. Two governors were forced to leave office. Evan Mecham was elected governor in 1986. He soon became known as a racist because he canceled the Martin Luther King Jr. holiday. His decision led to protests. Several businesses moved events to other states. Mecham also offended many ethnic groups and women with his statements. In 1988, Mecham was removed from office for misuse of public funds.

Arizona's State Government

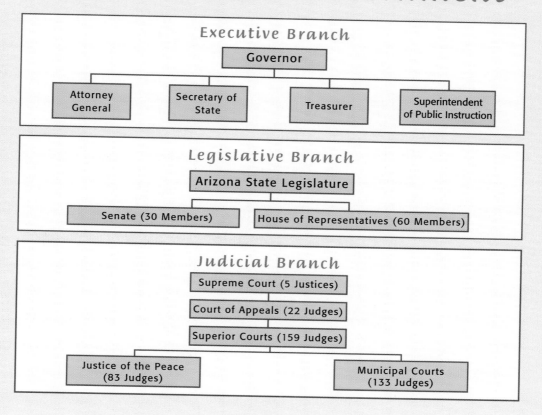

Executive Branch

Governor

Attorney General | Secretary of State | Treasurer | Superintendent of Public Instruction

Legislative Branch

Arizona State Legislature

Senate (30 Members) | House of Representatives (60 Members)

Judicial Branch

Supreme Court (5 Justices)

Court of Appeals (22 Judges)

Superior Courts (159 Judges)

Justice of the Peace (83 Judges) | Municipal Courts (133 Judges)

Businessman Fife Symington became governor in 1991. Four years later, he was elected to a second term. Symington was charged with bank fraud and not paying debts from his businesses. A federal court found him guilty of these charges. He resigned from office in 1997.

Arizona has also had many well-respected politicians. A famous Republican senator from Arizona was Barry Goldwater. He was elected to the U.S. Senate in 1952 and served until his retirement in 1986. He opposed federal government control. Goldwater wanted states to have more control over the laws they made. He was known for speaking his mind bluntly.

Goldwater ran in the 1964 presidential election. He lost to Lyndon Johnson by 16 million votes. Several years after the election, he said about his loss, "I've often said if I didn't know the Goldwater of 1964—and had to depend on the

Barry Goldwater was a respected politician from Arizona. He ran for president in 1964.

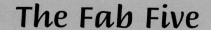

The Fab Five

In 1998, Arizona voters elected women to the state's top five offices. This was the first time this many top offices in a state have been held by women. People called the women the "Fab Five." Jane Hull, pictured, was the first woman to be elected Arizona's governor. Attorney General Janet Napolitano was the only Democrat among the five. The secretary of state was Betsey Bayless, the state treasurer was Carol Springer, and the superintendent of public instruction was Lisa Graham Keegan.

press—I'd have voted against...myself." Goldwater died in 1998.

Another famous Republican senator from Arizona is John McCain. McCain was elected to the Senate in 1985. He has fought for changes in campaign finance laws. McCain wants to make it harder for candidates to accept money from wealthy corporations. He ran for president in 2000, but the Republican Party chose George W. Bush over him.

Miranda Rights

In 1963, a truck driver named Ernesto Miranda, pictured on the right, kidnapped and raped an 18-year-old woman. After he was caught, he confessed to the crime. He was sentenced to serve 20 to 30 years in prison.

Two Phoenix lawyers appealed the sentence. They argued that police officers should have told Miranda that he had the right to remain silent as they arrested him. They argued that he should have had the opportunity to talk to a lawyer before police questioned him.

The case went to the U.S. Supreme Court in 1966. The court agreed with the two lawyers. It overturned Miranda's conviction. He received a new trial. The jury convicted Miranda of the crime based on other evidence. But because of that Supreme Court ruling, police officers now read a "Miranda rights" warning to anyone they arrest.

America's Toughest Sheriff

Sheriff Joe Arpaio of Maricopa County has been called "America's toughest sheriff." He became sheriff in 1993. He has started several new programs that are tough on criminals and help prevent crime. He outlawed cigarettes, R-rated movies, and coffee in the county's jails.

Prisoners in Maricopa County eat green bologna sandwiches and wear pink underwear. The meat's green color comes from being out in the air. Arpaio insists the bologna is safe and sometimes eats a sandwich to prove it. The pink underwear idea is to prevent people from stealing underwear and selling it on the streets as souvenirs. Arpaio wants prison conditions to be so bad that people will not want to go back to jail.

Arpaio also started using the famous "chain gangs" in Arizona. Five prisoners in a group are chained together by their ankles. They wear traditional black-and-white striped uniforms. They work six days a week. They sweep streets, remove graffiti, or clean up church lawns. Discipline is strict on these chain gangs. If an inmate swears, he has to do 50 push-ups.

Many people come to Arizona to enjoy year-round outdoor activities. Tourism is a large part of the state's economy.

Chapter 5

Economy and Resources

Arizona's beautiful weather and scenery are its most important natural resources. The warm winter weather draws people to the state. Many people escape cold climates and live in Arizona only during winter. During Arizona's hot summer, they return to their other homes. Arizonans call these people "snowbirds."

The warm weather has also attracted businesses. Companies may start their business in Arizona to draw employees who want to work in a warm climate.

Arizona's natural beauty draws millions of tourists every year. Tourists visit the state and spend their money at hotels, resorts, and restaurants. They add money to the state's economy.

Service Industries

Service industries are the largest industries in Arizona. They include health care, real estate, retail trade, and restaurants. As the state's population grows, real estate is becoming a major service industry. As more people move to Arizona, they are building more houses and businesses. In the past few years, Arizona's construction industry has boomed. Construction accounted for 7.4 percent of the state's jobs in 2001.

People used to think of Arizona as a wasteland. Today, the tourism industry continues to increase. Millions of people visit Arizona's national parks and other attractions every year. Tourism brings about $12 billion into the state each year.

Mining and Manufacturing

Copper mining is historically a major industry in Arizona. The Great Depression (1929–1939) was hard on the economies of all states. When the United States entered World War II, the demand for copper increased and helped Arizona's economy recover. Today, Arizona produces most of

Bisbee Deportation

In the past, copper mining was dangerous work. Miners risked cave-ins, fires, and large machinery accidents. During World War I (1914–1918), the copper industry boomed. Mining companies made millions of dollars from the sale of copper mined in Arizona.

Workers at that time were paid low wages and worked long hours. Miners in Bisbee tried to form a union and protest their working conditions. In 1917, half of the miners in Bisbee went on strike. Other people in Bisbee were against the strike and against the miners' union. Some of these people formed a group that forced 1,186 miners at gunpoint to get onto a train. The train took the miners to a remote desert area in New Mexico and left them there. The U.S. Army later rescued the miners. This event became known as the Bisbee Deportation.

the nation's copper. A major mining company called Phelps Dodge is based in Phoenix. Copper is used in plumbing, electrical wiring, cookware, and pennies.

Most of Arizona's manufacturing is in high technology products. Intel, a large company based in Chandler, makes

45

computer parts. Motorola, a company that produces cell phones and other communications products, is based in Tempe. Factories in the Phoenix area make aircraft parts.

Agriculture

Only about one-eighth of Arizona's land is suitable for farming. The amount of farmland depends on water available for irrigation. In desert areas, a hard layer of soil lies under the

topsoil. Called caliche, this layer is as hard as concrete and prevents farmers from growing crops.

Heat-loving crops grow well in Arizona's warm climate. During summer, farmers grow cotton in south-central Arizona, between Phoenix and Tucson. Lettuce is grown during winter in southwestern Arizona. Yuma holds a celebration called Lettuce Days every January.

Cotton and other southern crops grow well in Arizona's warm climate.

American Indians are Arizona's earliest people. Twenty-one Indian nations live in Arizona.

Chapter 6

People and Culture

American Indians lived in Arizona thousands of years before Spanish and other European settlers came. Today, more than one-fourth of Arizona's land is covered by Indian reservations. Twenty-one American Indian nations live in the state.

American Indians

The largest American Indian group in Arizona is the Navajo Nation. The Navajo have kept close ties to their land. They are known for raising sheep, goats, and horses. They also weave beautiful rugs. The Navajo reservation takes up most of northeastern Arizona and reaches into New Mexico and Utah. It is the largest Indian reservation in the country.

"Sheep are our life."
    —a saying of the Arizona Navajo, known for their traditional lifestyle

The Hopi reservation is inside the Navajo reservation. The Hopi live in villages on top of three mesas. One village, Oraibi, is the oldest continually inhabited settlement in the United States. The Hopi live simply, farming the dry land.

Other American Indian groups in Arizona include the Apache and the Tohono O'odham. The Apache have special ties to the mountains of central Arizona. Elders tell stories that took place in the mountains. The stories teach Apache children the values of their culture. The O'odham live in the Sonoran Desert. Water is important to these desert farmers. Their beliefs and ceremonies celebrate rain.

Hispanics

Before 1848, Arizona was part of Mexico. Many Mexicans traveled north to settle the area. Today, Hispanic influence in the state is strong. In public places, especially in southern Arizona, people speak both English and Spanish.

Many people in Arizona celebrate Cinco de Mayo, Las Posadas, and other Hispanic holidays. Cinco de Mayo, or May 5, honors the Mexican victory over the French in the

Arizona's Ethnic Background

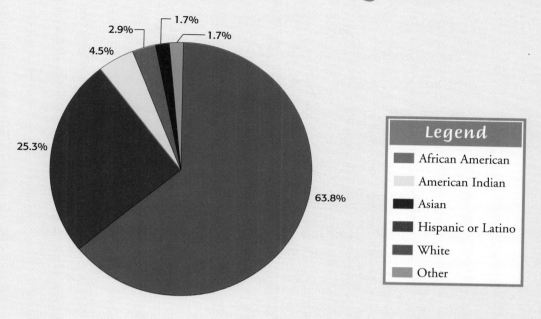

Legend
- African American
- American Indian
- Asian
- Hispanic or Latino
- White
- Other

1.7%
1.7%
2.9%
4.5%
25.3%
63.8%

Battle of Puebla in 1862. Las Posadas on December 16 is a Christian holiday that marks Joseph and Mary's trip to Bethlehem.

In some parts of Phoenix and Tucson, large, colorful wall paintings on the sides of buildings honor Hispanic heritage. These murals may be of famous Mexican Americans or contain religious symbols. The paintings are often short-lived. A mural might fade, or people might paint a new mural over an old one.

Weather Affects Lifestyles

Weather affects activities in Arizona. When the state got a professional baseball team, the Diamondbacks, it had to build a new stadium. Arizona decided to build a ballpark with air conditioning and a movable roof. At the new Bank One Ballpark in Phoenix, games could be played in the summer heat. Other major league baseball teams also take advantage of the warm spring weather. They hold spring training in Arizona.

Weather affects people's lives, too. Many people in desert areas have swimming pools in their yards. Golf is a favorite sport in Arizona. People play golf year-round.

Suburban Growth

The Phoenix suburbs of Mesa, Tempe, and Scottsdale are growing fast. Most people who move to the Phoenix area live in these suburbs. People are building new houses and businesses farther from downtown Phoenix. This kind of growth is called "suburban sprawl."

While Arizona faces the challenges of growth, it draws people with its colorful views and its booming economy. From snowy peaks to saguaro cacti that spread their arms above the desert, Arizona offers many opportunities to explore.

Bank One Ballpark in Phoenix has a movable roof and air conditioning, so people can play or watch baseball in hot weather. The stadium is often called "BOB."

Recipe: Fruit Salsa

Salsa is a popular southwestern snack. Wear rubber gloves when you handle jalapeno peppers. The hot juices from the peppers can hurt your skin.

Ingredients

1 14-ounce (420-gram) can of diced tomatoes
1 small jalapeno pepper, seeded and minced
½ medium white onion, chopped
1 average bunch of cilantro
2 oranges
½ teaspoon (0.5 mL) salt
½ teaspoon (0.5 mL) black pepper
bag of tortilla chips

Equipment

can opener
medium bowl
rubber gloves
cutting board
knife
large spoon
measuring spoon

What You Do

1. Open the can of diced tomatoes and pour it into the medium bowl.

2. Wearing rubber gloves, add the jalapeno pepper and onion.

3. Stir the mix with the spoon.

4. Remove the stems from the cilantro and chop it into small pieces.

5. Peel and cut the oranges into small pieces.

6. Add the cilantro and oranges to the mix.

7. Add salt and pepper to the mix.

8. Stir the mix with the spoon.

9. Serve with tortilla chips.

Makes 10-12 servings

Arizona's Flag and Seal

Arizona's Flag

The 13 stripes on the top of Arizona's flag stand for the 13 original American colonies. The stripes are designed to look like a sunset. The blue on the bottom is the same as in the U.S. flag. The copper star in the center stands for Arizona's copper mines.

Arizona's State Seal

The mountains and sunrise in the state seal represent the landscape of Arizona. The dam, lake, and irrigated field show that Arizonans have to water their land to grow crops. The miner with a pick and shovel represents the importance of mining to the state. The state motto "Ditat Deus" means "God enriches."

Almanac

General Facts

Nickname: Grand Canyon State

Population: 5,130,632 (U.S. Census 2000)
Population rank: 20th

Capital: Phoenix

Largest cities: Phoenix, Tucson, Mesa, Glendale, Scottsdale, Chandler

Agriculture

Agricultural products: Lettuce, cotton, citrus fruits, cattle, dairy products

Climate

Average winter temperature: 43 degrees Fahrenheit (6 degrees Celsius)

Average summer temperature: 78 degrees Fahrenheit (26 degrees Celsius)

Average annual precipitation: 13 inches (32 centimeters)

Geography

Area: 114,006 square miles (295,276 square kilometers)
Size rank: 6th

Highest point: Humphreys Peak, 12,633 feet (3,851 meters) above sea level

Lowest point: Colorado River, 70 feet (21 meters) above sea level

Cactus wren

Saguaro cactus blossom

Natural resources:
Climate, copper, turquoise, forests

Types of industry: Copper mining, computers and electronics, transportation equipment, chemicals manufacturing, tourism

Amphibian:
Arizona treefrog

Bird: Cactus wren

Fish: Apache trout

Flower: Saguaro cactus blossom

Gemstone: Turquoise

Mammal: Ringtail

Neckwear: Bola tie

Reptile: Arizona ridgenose rattlesnake

Song: "Arizona," by Margaret R. Clifford

Tree: Palo verde

First governor:
George W.P. Hunt

Statehood:
February 14, 1912 (48th)

U.S. Representatives: 6

U.S. Senators: 2

U.S. Electoral votes: 8

Counties: 15

Timeline

1400
The Anasazi and Hohokam civilizations disappear.

1680
American Indians fight the Spanish in the Pueblo Revolt.

1821
Mexico declares independence from Spain and claims parts of Arizona.

1848
The Treaty of Guadalupe–Hidalgo makes most of Arizona part of the United States.

1863
Arizona becomes a U.S. territory.

1620
Pilgrims establish a colony in the New World.

1775–1783
American colonists and the British fight the Revolutionary War.

1812–1814
The United States and Britain fight the War of 1812.

1846–1848
The United States and Mexico fight the Mexican War.

1861–186
The North the South fi the Civil W

1912

On February 14, Arizona becomes the 48th state.

1942–1945

Japanese Americans are sent to two camps in Arizona.

1973

Central Arizona project begins.

1934

Arizonan A. J. Eddy invents the evaporative cooler.

1998

Five women are elected to top state offices.

1914–1918

World War I is fought. The United States enters the war in 1917.

1939–1945

World War II is fought; the United States enters the war in 1941.

1964

U.S. Congress passes the Civil Rights Act, which makes discrimination illegal.

1929–1939

The Great Depression causes people to lose jobs.

2001

On September 11, terrorists attack the World Trade Center and the Pentagon.

Words to Know

butte (BYOOT)—a rocky hill with steep sides and a flat top

evaporative cooler (uh-VAP-or-uh-tiv KOOL-uhr)—a device that cools homes and businesses using water mist and dry air

gorge (GORJ)—a deep valley with steep, rocky sides

irrigation (ihr-uh-GAY-shuhn)—supplying water to crops using channels or pipes

mesa (MAY-suh)—a hill with steep sides and a flat top; mesas are common in southwestern deserts.

missionary (MISH-uh-ner-ee)—a person sent by a church or religious group to teach their beliefs in foreign lands

petrified forest (PET-ri-fyed FOR-ist)—trees that turned into stone

plateau (pla-TOH)—an area of high, flat land

reservation (rez-er-VAY-shun)—an area of land set aside by the U.S. government for American Indians

reservoir (REZ-ur-vwar)—a natural or artificial lake that holds a large amount of water

To Learn More

Blashfield, Jean F. *Arizona*. America the Beautiful. New York: Children's Press, 2000.

McDaniel, Melissa. *Arizona*. Celebrate the States. Tarrytown, N.Y.: Benchmark Books, 2000.

Murray, Stuart. *Wild West*. Eyewitness Books. London, New York: DK, 2001.

Wukovits, John F. *Wyatt Earp*. Legends of the West. Philadelphia: Chelsea House, 1997.

Internet Sites

Track down many sites about Arizona.
Visit the FACT HOUND at *http://www.facthound.com*

IT IS EASY! IT IS FUN!
1) Go to *http://www.facthound.com*
2) Type in: 0736815716
3) Click on "FETCH IT" and
   FACT HOUND will find several
   links hand-picked by our editors.

Relax and let our pal FACT HOUND do the research for you!

Places to Write and Visit

Arizona Historical Society Museum
949 East Second Street
Tucson, AZ 85719

Arizona Office of Tourism
2702 North Third Street, Suite 4015
Phoenix, AZ 85004

Arizona–Sonora Desert Museum
2021 North Kinney Road
Tucson, AZ 85743

Desert Botanical Garden
1201 North Galvin Parkway
Phoenix, AZ 85008

Governor of Arizona
1700 West Washington Street
Phoenix, AZ 85007

Grand Canyon National Park
P.O. Box 129
Grand Canyon, AZ 86023

Petrified Forest National Park
P.O. Box 2217
Petrified Forest National Park, AZ 86028

Colorful rocks like this one, called "The Wave," make the landscape of northern Arizona unforgettable.

Index

agriculture, 46–47
Anasazi, 20, 21–22
Apache, 22, 27–29, 50
Arizona Rangers, 29
Arpaio, Joe, 41

Bank One Ballpark, 52, 53
Bisbee Deportation, 45
buttes, 10

Carson, Colonel Kit, 27
Central Arizona Project, 33
climate, 16, 17–18
Cochise, 28–29
Colorado Plateau, 9–13
Colorado River, 5, 10, 30
Colorado River Compact, 30
copper, 44–45

Diamondbacks, 52

Earp, Wyatt, 26
Eddy, A.J., 30
evaporative cooler, 30–31

Fab Five, 39
farming. See agriculture
flag, 55
Flagstaff, 6, 10, 12

Gadsden Purchase, 27
Geronimo, 28, 29
Gila monster, 18, 19
Goldwater, Barry, 38–39
government, branches of, 35–36
Grand Canyon, 4, 5–6, 10, 22

Gunfight at the O.K. Corral, 26

Hispanic, 50–51
Hohokam, 21–22
Hopi, 21, 23, 50
Humphreys Peak, 10

internment camps, 32–33

Japanese Americans, 32–33

Kino, Father Eusebio Francisco, 23–24

Long Walk, 27
Lopez de Cardenas, Garcia, 22

manufacturing, 45–46
Maricopa County, 36, 41
McCain, John, 39
Mecham, Evan, 36
mesa, 10, 50
Mexican War, 25–26
mining 44–45
Miranda Rights, 40
Mogollon Rim, 12–13
Monument Valley, 8, 10
mural, 51

Navajo, 22, 27, 49
Navajo Indian Reservation, 10, 49

Painted Desert, 10
Petrified Forest, 10
Phoenix, 6, 15, 17, 19, 34, 36, 45, 46, 47, 51, 52, 53

Pima, 22, 23, 24
Pueblo Revolt, 23

ridgenose rattlesnake, 18
ringtail, 19
Roosevelt Dam, 30, 31

saguaro cactus, 14–15, 53
Salt River Canyon, 12, 13
San Francisco Peaks, 10
seal, 55
service industries, 44
Seven Cities of Cibola, 22
snowbirds, 43
Sonoran Desert, 9, 14, 15, 18, 50
Spanish missionaries, 23–24, 25
suburban sprawl, 53
Sun City, 33
Symington Fife, 37

Tohono O'odham, 22, 50
tourism, 42, 43, 44
Transition Zone, 9, 13
Treaty of Guadalupe-Hidalgo, 25–26
Tubac, 24

Valley of the Sun, 15
Vasquez de Coronado, Francisco, 22, 23

Webb, Del, 33
White Mountains, 13
wildlife, 18–19
Wild West, 27–29
World War II, 31–32